The Seasons are Over

and

The Paradox

To Susan,
My everlasting friend.

W Calvin Brown
Nov. 2 2005

The Seasons are Over

and

The Paradox

Poems by
W. Calvin Brown

Copyright © 1996, 2000 by W. Calvin Brown

All rights reserved.
No part of this book may be reproduced, stored in a retrieval system, or transmitted by any means, electronic, mechanical, photocopying, recording, or otherwise, without written permission from the author.

ISBN: 1-58820-012-4

This book is printed on acid free paper.

1stBooks – rev. 11/9/00

To Helen, my wife

> To Silvia, Stephanie and Shirley -- without
> Whose patience, tolerance, and affection
> These words would not have been possible.

Table of Contents

	Page
South of the Track	1
The Final Search	3
Feeling the Soul	5
Give of Himself	7
The Letter-Carrier's Farewell	9
Love is No More	11
The Passing Away	13
A Custodian's Prayer	15
The Lost Art	17
The Infidel	19
The Tiff of Nature	21
Pain	23
Dead Eyes	25
Ephemeral	27
All Must Fade	29
Nature's Secret	31
The Infant Old Man	33
Loves Behind Me	35
Selling the Human	37
Men of Steel	39
The Last Call	41
To Helen:	43
The Withered Sword	45
Parents, Sir, I Had None	47
Fighting the End	49
A Friend is Any Man	51
To My Mother	53
TRIBUTE TO A READING RECOVERY TEACHER	55
A TRIBUTE TO GEORGE THE BUILDER	57
Frailty	59
His Forgiveness	61

No One to Call Mine	63
Birth is All Mine	65
The Last Autumn	67
Season's End	69
Face of Death	71
Call of The Ocean	73
God's Ecstasy	75
Fools for Love	77
The Ever Ticking Clock	79
Visit From Nature	81
I Follow Thee	83
Love, By Law	85
Forbidden Love	87
Greatness Unearned	89

South of the Track

Borne, yet a boy ---south of the track,
With a rugged nose and skin of black;
Did childish things as children do,
Wore ragged clothes that to me seemed new;
Second-rate books---I carried on my back;
Due to my birth---south of the track!

I remembered places I was forbidden to go,
A swimming-pool---even church or a picture show;
With bold letters---NO COLORED ALLOWED!
What unfortunate fate had I endowed?
In fear---I accepted this lawful fact,
I remembered my place---south of the track!

In my youth, I could not understand,
Where was my place in America's plan?
With a Constitution of flimsy laws,
Contractual promises full of flaws,
Ambition I had---but chances I lack;
Because I was born---south of the track!

As I grew older I went to war,
What then was I fighting for?
A piece of land----an executive post;
Freedom, my friend---was denied me most.
But memories returned me to that shack;
Picked up, where I left---south of the track!

Now, I am old, I have no regret,
Have witnessed a sunrise---watched it set;
No matter where you are in nature's game,
Its beauty is there and all the same.
I gathered God's glories in my opened pack,
And remained in freedom---south of the track!

The Final Search

Sometimes on the road and around the bend,
Is a light I never see.
On the horizon at the rainbow's end,
Is a pot not meant for me.
There is no pier on which to rest my ore,
From that daily task at sea.
There is only that love of yesteryore,
That left its embrace for me.
I've found no slumber in this early flight,
Nor dreams that could set me free.
Upon this dark...dark earth, there is no light,
To behold eternity.
I've finally ascended to heaven's door,
Here was that light...I've been searching for...

Feeling the Soul

Have you not heard a thousand silent whispers
When the sun is hidden betwixt the poles?
Feeling how restless 'bout our bodies that slumbers
To give nightly freedom to these anxious souls.
Have I not felt this soul aspore in madness
Infested by hatred and pangs afresh?
When met the dawn...and returned in sadness,
Resiled and dwelled around this putrid flesh.
Have I not rendered commiseration
For this fretful spirit in each thy bone?
Despising this court of fratinization,
Receiving no rest until it stands alone...
Alas! Death doth summons thee unto its route;
Then my soul, in freedom, will remain without.

Give of Himself

A man in need by the side of the road,
Peering upward from his humble abode,
Begging each man as he passed his way,
For needed gifts that would bless his day,
First came the rich who would offer his coin,
Then came the farmer who would fatten his loin.
I need neither money nor food said he,
But something unmeasured, you could give to me.
Perplexed they were by this stubborn man,
Who refused this blessing from their gentle hand;
But little they knew, they could simply give
To a vexed man who just wanted to live...
Not just the fortune he would eventually spend,
Not just the food that would ultimately end,
But that gift stored in one's heart on the shelf
He wanted a man "To give of himself".

The Letter-Carrier's Farewell

What manner and breed of men are we?
Whose forceful footsteps never cease;
Where trodded pavement wears from years
And from day to day we take our lease;
Who walks beneath a blistering sun...
A journey that makes him feel alone.
So sleeps the world when his day's begun,
Yet smiles...at troubles of his own;
Carriers of joy and often pain,
Smiles with the rich...cries with the poor
Shuns the wind and ignores the rain,
With special problems from door to door
The bell has summoned my last plight
And now my daily toil is through,
Like a tired old bird that sinks in flight
Now perches on trees...over once he flew.
The journey gets weak from waning years,
And the final curtain must fall.
I say, farewell to you...my peers
And hang my satchel upon the wall.
This is a scene that we all must play
In declining years from day to day.
The drama is over and all is done
We shall all come to pass...
one by one.

Love is No More

When every love and all its joy is bent from me,
My impatient heart is stoopt and seeks no more
To find its resting comfort that oft' might enthrone me
With her unrooted passion that this loin did implore,
With a heated tongue that cries to be kissed
With limped breast that are fallowed and unrobed,
With a warm bosom where pinning is ne'er desist,
With a love where once thy love had its abode,
With Nature where no raiments are covered o'er
With subversive acts devised from all within,
Where least the body's chamber has ne'er an encore,
And called chaste by a lover...but life...by men.
Oh! Taketh of what thy lover is bodily giving
For this be the life and the use of my living.

The Passing Away

Many a waxing sunset have I seen,
Slowly departing from its chamber;
Yet so swiftly and hastily we past between...
From life to death's perennial slumber.
How gentle and permanent seems the rain
That never ceases 'twixt night and day;
And yet our half-nurtured lives contain
A brisk and rapid..."passing away"...
Fixed is the beauty of a child's first song
With lasting jingles from men of yore;
Yet our bones silently sprint along;
A speedy second and is seen no more.
Oh! How lasting the beauty of Nature's hand,
How swift my journey to God's fair land...

A Custodian's Prayer

Lord, please hear this custodial plea
With sweet deliverance that will set me free;
Let me leave these indelible scars,
Away from this hall...and loading cars.

Deliver me from these marked up doors,
And stains of coffee upon my floors;
Take me from this beck -and- call;
An accident brewing in the hall.

Gum and crayons whenever able,
Will always end beneath a table.
Set me free from these janitor's codes
Of leaky roofs and obstructed commodes.
Deliver me from this fiendish, yet angelic cry,
From hell's little saints as they pass me by.

God-like prints in remote places,
Demon smiles upon their faces.
Yet, remember...in this tutorial trod
These little creatures belong to God.
Things would be different---if I would dare
Bring back the words of a simple prayer.

Yet many phases make such beauty
When a man might smile and do his duty.
I don't move as agile as before,
And it takes me longer to sweep a floor.
My broom is withered; the straw is worn...
I await the summons of Gabriel's horn.

I shall answer by and by;
I'll seek that building in the sky.
And if someone should ask if I am around,
Please answer---in a reverent sound,

"We saw him last...seeking a hug,
And someone swept him beneath the rug."

For old custodians never die... they just get swept away.

The Lost Art

And in the dampness of my cell
Where books lay ragged and papers torn;
Beneath the gutters of my dell,
I once lay infant and yet unborn...
Where eridites once had foolish wits
Or artists with brushes and yet no scene;
Or the writer who wrote...but now just sits
And ponders o'er a plot that once he'd seen...
"Tis life itself that makes me fool
And scan the canopy of my grave,
Where Nature entwines me 'bout his spool
And nurtures thy sleep within my cave.
And yet it broils me from the least of aught...
I find me useless, but yet unfraught.

The Infidel

Frailty of man destine by Nature's brink
With pervertic morals and natural instinct
To travel the road as an infidel
Shunning the laws that marriage upheld
The male of the species since yester-years
Leaving his mate in raging tears.
He's endowed to say "yes"...his heart says "no",
Falling to nature and master of his show
Aggressive we are; we must play our fate,
Insatiable duty from mate to mate.
If women would forgive and understand
It was not my choice that I am a man,
From what if any should you measure my worth...
Surely not my weakness...blame my birth.

The Tiff of Nature

When the tiff of Nature is drunken o'er
And ghostly spirits stagger o'er the lea,
And sluggish trees sway from Nature's door
In violent rage it comes to thee
I've seen this madness about its womb
With tears that flooded the antique shores,
That faulted and sank into its tomb
Where Nature staves the silence of its chores.
I've heard his bellow from yonder sphere
With cruel laughter---breaking a silent night;
And petulant winds devoid of fear
Traveling unsobered and marveling its might.
And all this thou master overturns---
On the path of madness, it oft' sojourns.

Pain

I wonder how gentle this death should rise
When life's physical pain is fore'er strong;
'Tis a wonder how patient it ever lies,
Awaiting its plunge---with darkness along---
'Tis in askance, I find, this journey---death,
Whether 'tis pain or fright of the after-breath;
Afraid that all is forever done,
That life and death are a single one;
Such final pain, it summons thee;
For I must answer its silent toll,
And this life-like dream is taken from me,
Awakening the sickness of my soul ---
So gently its saber is thrust within me;
So swiftly is judgement cast upon me.

Dead Eyes

How often men with eyes do not see
The glorious blooming of a common rose,
Or the birth of a bud on a simple tree...
A cool, cool evening when the sun goes.
How unheard is the sound...and yet have ears...
The melody of the mockingbird's song,
Thundering sound of rain and mystic fears,
And a fleeting sunset that creeps along.
Do we feel the breath of the day's last touch?
And ignorant smiles that remain within,
'pon a perfect nature that gives too much
To those dead, dead souls of thankless men.
Yet ears that hear, hearts that feel, eyes that see;
This beauty, my friend, is freedom to me.

Ephemeral

W	What rapid scenes do this weary life possess?
I	In short performance my tale-told is done;
L	Like a brief day that suddenly makes agress,
L	Like brisk showers changing to smolten sun.
I	In the mist of dreams...Have been found a decade;
A	And found in sleep...An unexpected minute;
M	Making a life-ship...In one single parade.
C	Casting from its bra...Every soul within it.
B	Bound to its summons...To proscenium, I go!
R	Reborn with the audience, to oblivion below.
O	Oh! That this scene could forever grow.
W	Why do sudden plots conclude in reverence
N	Narrated and cultured by the audience?

All Must Fade

What if Nature's luxury would ever retain
Its silent mystery upon perfect beauty?
What if a rose, short-lived, could in sweetness remain
In pristine brightness, unlimp't above its duty?

Where is the rolling sea of the conquistador,
The luminent stars that guided me 'pon this land?
Where fables that crowded the hearts of yesteryore
Or the cautious robin that suppered from my hand?

Where is that greeting, where a smile was in fashion?
Where is that frosty river of the ancient shore?
Where is that bosom that was engulfed with passion?
Where is that traveling beggar upon my door?

Where is that courtier with his chivalrous cape,
Or the royal coachman with his courteous hand?
Where is that lucid beauty of the moon's fair shape,
Surrounded by immanent stars of yester-land?

What extinguished the embers of your lover's loins?
And where is the temperance of Nature's fair breast?
Where is the God-like richness of a Roman coin,
Or lasting love and church-hood so patiently at rest?

Where is the moody artist and his Godly scene?
Where lies the leafy flora that was once of green?
Oh! That beauty's stillness could be forever upborne,
Where each new life would be permanently adorne.

I would feign to see this speedy blessing reposed
And this death of beauty would be staved and then
All Nature's enigma would then remain unclosed,
And all our hearts will be rested as patient men.

Nature's Secret

I have seen by Nature's sunlight
A brilliance that never unfold
The mystery of my short flight
Or the essence of ny soul.
Never pending to e'er impart
What ends my ;destiny will meet
And never saying in hell thy art
Or Heaven...to no man shall greet.
Just to say wither thou goest
When everything lives but thy breath,
In truth, I feel that thy knowest
That there belives some after-death.
And yet these years get centuries old
Waiting Nature...its gems...unfold...

The Infant Old Man

We are all children, brief with time and age;
Our minds unchanged as we turn our page,
Possessed with fear and fancies unseen,
Yet gray hair and spectacles in between.
What makes us wiser than the newborn child?
When it is gentle and we so wild.
We fret, we smile, we often find,
Just like that child we left behind.
We return to the crib...just bigger in size,
So often forgetful to realize,
Again we are pampered in that fleeting minute,
Holding on to life and all that's in it.
Only years grow old in this human game,
But our moving follies remain the same...

Loves Behind Me

And all ills are faltering far behind me,
Where once I lay born with dreams to remind me;
Where every awl has staved to kill or find me,
Where day's blessings embroils do entwine me,
Where Nature's halter did long to bind me,
Where death did summons and its master did sign me,
Where every grain of soil pierced and grind me,
Where the heart is silent...cadavers do line me,
Where my lover's loves are passions to supine me,
Where my lover's loins do seek to pine me,
Where the devil's venomous trident is led to chine me,
No longer do my wits live to remind me;
In solace, I rest, and in darkness you'll find me...

Selling the Human

Red and pale'd
Yet never fail'd
To stand 'fore me on the block,
Touch't my skin
That crawl'd within
To test the purchase of this stock.

Human tool
Devoid of school
Yet, precious, the black of beast
Morning sun
His day begun
And bloody soil work't his lease.

Blistered hands
From antique lands
Mark this drama upon the stage
Faces that cry
Before they die
Forcing their souls to another age.

Men of Steel

To Vesuvius' conquers, to men of steel,
To men whose brows are scortch'd and tan'd,
To the architects of cannons...of the sailors' keel,
Makers of lava from an angry hand,
To the whiskered men who have labored at hell's front door,
And to those whose guts have been burned,
To the ladleman, the moulder, melters of ore,
To the kokeman, craneman, all those concern,
To the open hearth, the furnace, the cupelo,
To the bath, the ladle, and the bail,
To the smolten pits where many have sunken belo'.
Beneath the girdle of nature's vail,
To the steel men of silence to men of renown,
I give thee my blessings...a golden crown.

The Last Call

I've seen the top , had riches and gold;
Never was hungry and never was cold.
I found that pot at the rainbow's end,
Coins and dollars at the road's bend.

I grew old in grace and perfect glory,
Thanking no one for this perfect story.
I've purchased the best that money could buy,
Not thinking of destiny...or that I would die.

Oh, how pompous, when I shouted aloud,
To the humble souls, the impoverished crowd
I need you not, I can stand on my own,
I beg nobody, I can live alone.

And now I am near my day of death
With plenty of money, but short on breath.
I am now in need at the end of my trod;
I was all alone...so I called on God...

To Helen:

H	How often in silence have I thought,
E	Engulfed with the presence of all our ways.
L	Love and joy that you have brought,
E	Enduring the pain of our darkest days,
N	Not ignoring the wisdom...you have taught.
M.	Many moments remind me...of your strength behind me.
B	Bright were some days of our many years,
R	Remembering some sad ones that passed us by.
O	Oh! The obstacles you conquered without any fears,
W	Weathering the storms without a cry.
N	Now love is greatest...in the autumn of our years.

                                          Your Husband

                                          Billy
                                          1990

The Withered Sword

I watched her pantalets fall to the green land
And her raw flesh lay blushing, waiting 'pon it,
And touching this bosom with my gentle hand
Ascended the glory to nature's summit
'Pon the cold, cold earth did two warm souls combine
Like a nurtured babe upon maternal breast.
Two tongues like rogues in their prison confine,
And the sword in its sheath and here does it rest.
Oh, were this death, then the dead be abliss
For she dies a million and one sweet pains,
And we in pantaloons die once of this,
As nature bequeaths upon us crutches and canes.
Our valliant swords are withered...so they seem,
But the shame of the sheath pines another theme.

Parents, Sir, I Had None

Parents, sir, I had none,
Absent years...one by one;
No hand to show me how,
Or wipe tears from my brow.

How rich the crime upon the street,
Leaves and smoke to make it sweet.
Kill, or not to kill...'thought a tear.
Stand alone, by my gun,
Parents, sir, I had none.

Yet, happy limit of my time,
A common peer, I'd often find
An enemy---much like me,
And face to face--we meet our grace.
For his gun is ready like mine.
Parents, sir, there are none for me.

What's it like, the other road?
Things I wished I'd had,
A pat on the head---is often said,
The stormy voice of a dad,
This, I miss, just a kiss
Parents, sir , I never had.

I lack the glory in their voice,
I am here, not by choice.
Bodies lay --- who must pay,
For their throwing me away?
You see, they're just like me
No parents, in their day.

It all done, this lonely strife,
The short days, I called life.
I met my foe---it's time to go,

In the gutter, streets below,
Ended my quest---in silent rest,
With a bullet in my chest.
In silent whisper from the grave, it's done,
Parents, sir, I had none.

Fighting the End

Oh! Death! That I could be the lasting sun
Painted eternally over these bones,
That has shone its brilliance since time's begun
Never ceasing to melt these rugged stones.
If I could stave the cloak of thy darkness
With a flashing golden bar of sunlight
And leave thee barren, lifeless, and harkness.
Unable to impugn this speedy flight.
Oh! Death! That summons thee and quiet too soon
I find me covered o'er 'neath thy abyss...
Casted low from nature's relentless 'goon
And cheated of life and eternal bliss;
That I could pass from this lonely minute
And watch this world sunken with you in it.

A Friend is Any Man

I met a man whose face was black,
Who lived in slums across the track,
Whom I was taught to face with fear,
And be cautious of what I hear.

Never to touch his midnight skin,
Watch his moves that come from within...
About these to the man I said,
"I feel so close and not afraid."

I touched his hand and felt no pain,
Heard his deep voice without disdain,
Putting the test to all such men,
This black face is now my best friend.

Why so touched...that it set me right
Why tell this tale?...for I am white...

To My Mother

I recall the days of my childhood lare,
With every pain, she was always there...
Who'd patch my trousers and its worn-out seat;
Who unruffled my garments, made them neat,
And exhausted nights after worn-out fun,
She would tuck me in when my day is done.

Approaching the hill of becoming a man...
Remembering that touch as child-hood began
Still needing the music of her whispered tone
Letting me know, I was still not alone.
To touch her cheek seems oft' to remind me,
Of the lovable pleasures, left behind me.

'Tis in my mind... I shall not grow old,
Mother and child are one...so I am told.
When journey's end and under no care,
I'll reach for support, shel'll be standing there.

TRIBUTE TO A READING RECOVERY TEACHER

Coming to a land of different sound,
And yet we looked the same;
It was in our speaking that I soon found,
Different was my name.

The alphabet begins with "A" as mine -
"Simple," I thought to myself.
But starting this course from its prime,
Put doubt upon the shelf.
                Reading was the game;
                Sound was its name.

The Prediction of Progress, moved this course
With independent sound.
My reading and learning with gentle force,
Gave courage to stand my ground.

The many crude shapes of my lips and tongue,
made sounds, I never knew.
It's in blended sound, so the poets have sung,
Where we can read anew.
                Reading was the game;
                Sounds of letters is the fame.

So I learned my "ah's," and I learned my "oh's,"
By moving my ;tongue around
I could say "Thank you", and many "Hello's,"
By just reading common sounds.

It is day by day, I make my progress;
And twenty weeks of fun.
With confidence in me, and doubting less,
For reading is on the run.
                Reading was the game;

Sounds was its name.
Often, I wonder just where I would be,
If Reading Recovery were not here.
I would have no esteem within me,
And meeting kids in fear.

But now this joyful task is behind me,
And to the world I tell,
That often my gratitude reminds me -
of Knox and Raphael.
Reading was the game,
Sounds was its name.

A TRIBUTE TO GEORGE THE BUILDER

God gathered His materials with a mindful plan
With muscles and bones to make a man,
With a crude substance from this dead-like earth
He conceived a man in uncommon birth.

Said He to this man: I'll put you on trial
To prove yourself in a short while...
Make your destiny without a flaw,
Use your tools by my spiritual law.

He followed His spirit in the wanning years
Took all pain and dried his tears,
Stood on naked earth and read his plan
And started to build with hammer in hand.

Observing his prints from page to page,
Straightening up walls that were bent from age...
With perfection and skill one could see
The finished product as a temple should be.

Now he's wrapped in surrendering quilt;
Yet on every road there's a house he had built.
He's dropped his belt - for all is done;
He's driven his last nail - the battle is won.

We will not hear that sound anymore
Laying of tile - his hanging a door...
And even yet, it won't be the same
If we can't call our builder, George, by name.

The days are done - the sun is down;
He has answered the call of the trumpet's sound,
His hammer is silent, his tools are still;
He's contracted to heaven and destined to build.

When we hear the crash of thunder on a summer day
We could ponder in askance and simply say;
It's probably his golden hammer striking a cloud
Making sure his work is heavenly endouwed.

So long George, we shall always find
The beauty of your art - you left behind.

Frailty

How often does her womb lie untouched
By the flames that kindle in my loin,
With lusting embers, erected and uncrutched
And embroiled with desire to her bosom join.
When frigid breast lay limpid without its bra,
Awaiting the hands of my summer's heat
Allowing a perfect replica,
And forever meddle on her golden seat.
And yet each season leaves her garments worn
To satiate the lust of my breath
She slumbers with all and again upborn,
He fades in shame to his piteous death
'Tis the gentle woman of whom I speak
Who impugns the man and deems him weak.

His Forgiveness

And every pity's eye is teared upon Him
With excellent woes unstaved to encamp them;
By the interment He lies but grimly sees us,
We, who betrayed Him, the name of Jesus.
A mounted stone planted by His cave,
A rooted cross thus placed before His grave
Were the cruxes of this perplexed amiss
That murdered the pith of unseen bliss..
Who ascended to the bounds of Heaven's face
Engulf with pangs...yet a gentle grace;
But in these spirits do we humbly esteem
To love, be praise, to worship, to redeem....

No One to Call Mine

If men could see when love is done
And the moon refused to shine,
And hearts do falter one by one
With no one to call mine.

Can you not hear the melody
Where lovers only dine,
And ;yet I am all alone
With no one to call mine.

I am lost in this dark valley
With only love to find,
When my search is all done,
There's no one to call mine.

Birth is All Mine

Vexed was the fathom of the birth measured.
Mis-lead was the venture 'fore my prime,
yet in the knowing, 'twas all so pleasured ---
Though the day before was of dismal time.
And discomfort within my mother's womb,
I whined...yet tongueless\\\where silence did join---
And now her use is rested by her tomb
Where once I lay blooming within her loin.
Yet by the wisdom nature is to blame
For this corrupted flesh about her bones;
And yet His uses wonder---all the same
When life doth He gives; death He condones.
Thy mother and her's and her's before
Hath lived just to born me---nothing more.

The Last Autumn

When the last pansy is dip't beneath its bed
And every petal is drop't from its ill pith,
Then, rustle to the grave and conjoin the dead
And follow their kindred through its labyrinth;
When every tree yearns for a coat of bark
And its lofty branches shed its withered dress
That shield them from dew in the summer's dark
'Bove the paradise of lovers, where loves did confess
Each tiny creature that labored through nature's minute
And closes the floral windows of its cave
Where once 'old sol' had shown within it,
But now is a denizen outside its grave.
Thus the fortune of all growth is sunken by the sea
I await by the shores 'til it returns to me.

Season's End

When winter prinks the impetus of its cheerless breath
And receeds beyond the realm of frosty clouds,
It sends me kneeling before the use of its parried death
All blanket o'er with tears and purple shrouds.
As slained from war where oft' it had bidden
Not to subdue or injoin the arrival of the sun.
Yet, here, 'neath the abyss...its soul lies a 'hidden,
'Til it emits the ostent of its doing and done...
And gives way to fallowed soil where it would till
Or being marshalled to exit with the tears and chides.
'Tis never a bare tree that sheds as it will
Though its empty arms bathing where winter abides.
So, sob no more when its doing is amid and undone,
Each season sinks to its grave..one by one.

Face of Death

When nature's visor is lifted from its face,
And a vision of heaven looks upon me,
There lies in silence from its hidden grace.
Before it girdles my soul and steals it from me;
With gentle talons that claw the pith of my bones
And sweet pains impugn this worn-out flesh,
And nebulous dreams of mist seem real
When all sins have faded and hallow'd afresh.
A mysterious venom that had no sting,
Made its final summons to it s judgement seat.
What a glorious sound from the heavens ring;
I await the splendor of cadence of its beat.
Life is a mysterious dream, so I am told,
But in the face of death...al will unfold.

Call of The Ocean

'Tis the ocean that draws the death of men,
Who sink as they pray 'neath the mortis main,
With ripples that foist a deadly kin,
And floods the shores where men have lain.
A gentle flow...I've seen it roam,
Its lofty chamber from morn 'til dusk.
And enrobe the pebbles with its salted foam
And o'er flow the pansies and the earth encrust...
With a luminant moon that hangs above its thread
And clouds that entomb this tumulting flow
The lascars venomous arms reaching from its bed.
Reaching for men to bring them below.
When I am sunken 'neath the fathoms of the sea,
The anchor of the depths is fortune to me.

God's Ecstasy

Whilst an annealed breast did warm thy tongue,
As I lay near thy lover's loin,
More sweet yet bitter so lovers have sung
When their fervid bossoms lie ajoin.
With ragged raiments raffed...and thighs above
The sweetest flora from the scent of her flesh.
And the avarice in me whispered, she needs of love.
As I scan't with pine and desire afresh...
And two did lie no more the twain,
But breast to breast and brain to brain.
When nature deploys his wittiest delusion
That embroiled the souls to ill confusion;
But 'tis yet the brightest of the brightest sun,
When flesh is to flesh...then life is begun.

Fools for Love

When follies find me well at han'
And make me fool for thus,
Methinks I am the greater man
To suit my use upon thy trus'.
This office grants my life in vex
With obsequious thoughts, they perchance
Like those by the minister of his tex'
While bewildered sinners loose their glance.
When thou hath found on adultered kiss
Or the lifting spree of a pure embrace,
It troubles not the heartly bliss
That resteth lightly ;upon thou face.
When reality finds me 'pon thy cot,
'Twill find me saying, "I love...and I love not"...

The Ever Ticking Clock

'Tis in the time when stillness is unborn
And every degree doth staves to rest.
When every day's blessings might itself adorn
And present its drama with wanton guest.
When suns encroach their rental due,
And smolts the faculties of men,
They decline and break from nature's sinew
And stop, but sleepless...and again begin.
But through the winters and ne'er undone
Are the hands of nature's time
Who giveth as little to all and one...
From his ending...down to his prime.
Every life is brief and to hell or heaven...thus it sends...
But time is the drama that never ends.

Visit From Nature

Many roots have entwined beneath these eyes
And hath been smolten in the blistered sun
That drop their petals when the stem lies...
Beneath thy Autumn when their visits are done.
I've beheld the wreath of a defloating yawl
And a wake that girdled the keel of the earth
That nurtured the lascars with his precious awl,
and becomes the tanju o'er his restless berth...
Thus left them reaming to the keva of the deep
To be embalmed in the kloof of a gentle sleep
And yet many a summit have been increst'
That protrudes 'bove the wake of the sea
And I gad as fouls from nest to nest...
To accost this rampart that was lavished to thee.

I Follow Thee

Free me from these bonds of despair
So the pillage of my brain will steal no more
Your strength and power that defeat me there.
Lend me your crutch…I so implore;
Let all my weakness leave my soul.
That I could as thee be eager and fain
To change the status of my role.

Let my frailties turn love from pain
Yet then however you come to thee,
My failing heart then loves you still
And knowing by the clock as you know me,
I follow your guidance as ever I will.
Will follow you in the darkness of the night
Where I am a mere shadow in your fair light…

Love, By Law

Dare God of Nature pluck thy sense
Or say that love has recompense.
Real love has no charge from heart at all
Or is there judgement for its fall.
This love is free through instant glare,
Having God's touch that lingers there,
Yet lies the bonds to seek its lare...

> Many unsound loves have I seen
> And dying leaves that were once green,
> Endowed yet...by God in between.

Can you not see that love's alone?
Each kiss...to God...we must atone.
Pain for those who might this love scorn,
Had used the loins when love was unborn;
And this law shall fade behind me,
Seeking true love...thus I found thee.

Forbidden Love

When I must pause at the common laws
That keep me in my cave,
I feel the pain--of my disdain
That will take me to my grave.

There is a hand, I kiss as a man
That straightens the bend in the road.
The heart must turn--and often burn
When I arrive at my wretched abode.

Stars in our eyes, beneath the skies
Under this cloud, we sing aloud
Shouting in grace, our final place
And only lovers are allowed,
Never parting from Nature's face.

Greatness Unearned

What is it in this social game
That makes greatness with just a name?
Did nothing where he stood alone
No conquest--that was his own.
Behind the lines with a frightful few,
Earning metals as cowards do,
Inflated ego--expanded breast
Falsely standing with the rest,
With a flimsy urge to take first place
When he didn't even enter the race.
What glory there is to compete
For some who win is mere defeat.

The Paradox

The legal system in America is designed to promote a lucrative status for the judicial process.

The grandiloquent can turn injustice into doubt and guilt into innocence.

There is no wonder that the defense ignores the guilt of his client.

The defense will sleep uneasily before it closes the brief on its final case.

The mysterious drop of a single tear changes things.

The cascade voice of a wife's tongue could inundate the entire desert.

How frequently do we pursue the talent we don't have to ignore the one that God gave us.

Oh! How the overseer squeals "like a pig" when he feels the sting of the whip.

The curtain of life has risen; the stage is set for the performers and without rehearsal they play their parts.

In order that the aspiring plateau of life is reached, one must pass through many phases of imperfections.

The coward has plenty of experience in dying.

The death penalty is asylum for the murderer; keep him living for complete retribution.

Depression is an uncomfortable epidemic to those who neglect the medicine of faith.

I believe the unbelievable, touch the untouchable, see the unseeable, and grasp the hand of God.

Promiscuity is becoming more and more presidential, politicians indulge but they don't ejaculate.

Nature was created by God to give man his only; unconquerable challenge.

One can be rich without a penny when he smiles in the face of God.

Man is merely a grown boy who never found out how to unplug his choo choo train.

The more we try to live the less time we have to reckon with death.

Teenagers are mere babies who have grown whiskers long before puberty.

The function of a gun is to kill and man is a destined murderer.

The automobile is an uncontrolled weapon.

Stereotype is one picked from the vast minority and categorized in the vast majority.

Man considers all women vulnerable and possibly infidels– except his daughter.

A clock met with profound scrutiny, never ticks.

The rich and prestigious politition use the poor and insignificant to construct their power of a separate entity.

What an injustice to the lively rose; plucked, merely to be thrown upon the grave.

There is a sure way for a woman to cause a man to repudiate: keep saying "No"!

Wise men frown in the face of knowledge while fools find joy in the pitiful ignorant.

The only wrong that is surely to be forgiven and forgotten is the one that is never committed.

The nearly perfect thing about masturbation is that neither disease nor pregnancy can claim its results.

Man, the dog, would not be so crude, if there were not so many enchanting fire hydrants.

No one want s to die nor live forever.

Cowards lie in their graves long before the funeral.

The loud voice of faith can be heard the world over and yet one close by can hear it not.

How often do lovers stumble along the way and yet so seldom know it is love.

Some love is like a freshly plucked rose…brief in time before it fades.

An oppressed people will eventually destroy its government.

To embellish the body is to kill Nature. For is not the rose a cultivated weed; so then, if we move ourselves from bad ground, then in our own simple microcosm we, too, like the rose, are beautiful.

When man sees things that are not there, he hears things that have no sound; he feels things that have no touch, and he believes things that are unbelievable–then he has faith.

> The minister taught me to turn the other cheek,
> My mother taught me to fight and not be meek.
> My teacher bidded: Take it, and swallow the pill.
> The Army gave me a weapon by which to kill,
> Yet, now, I am fought by instructive illusion,
> For what they taught created perfect confusion.

I was in doubt about my mental stability until I engaged a psychologist–now I am certain.

Oh! How the slow moments of each hour speed the day with short years.

God is seldom late, but when He is, He is still on time.

From station to station, we are destined to play our part.

Diminish that stuff in the stomach and the heart has nothing to pump.

Love is inevitably true and inborn, but the acquisition of hate is taught.

Nature never borne a bad day. For every raindrop that splashes upon the umbrella, falls to the Earth to cultivate the rose.

intelligence is merely cultivated ignorance.

Before the student can propel through the rough waters of learning, the teacher must supply him with an adequate vessel.

The seed does not germinate because of the planter.

Imbued with complacency and felicity is the ignorant. Yet, on dangerous and pensive avenues travel the so called intelligent.

What if like the clam or oyster, we could change our sex to meet the need.

The devil need not solicit friendship, for he has a full house.

Then I scan a creature in duty's cause
Flickers for a minute in life-long pause;
The moth, aging to its greatest power
Yet flutters its wings for a fleeting hour.
How gently and gradual does nature bestow the beauty of youthful fertility upon us, and so suddenly steals it back.

The only difference between woman's loquacity and a violent rainstorm is that the storm will eventually end.

No where between the bridge of physical development of man and woman can we find a true being.

The genius will inevitably learn which makes teaching a comfortable institution...but a dedicated teacher must graciously encounter the ordeal of teaching the ignorant.

The only person who avows that the possession of money is the precipitant of damnation is the one who has none.

I would like to meet the man who could endure the quick pain of child-birth or the woman who could fulfill the blessed second with a pompous cigar.

Love is the natural growth that comes without cultivation; but hatred is that seedless ingredient that comes from fallowed soil.

There is nothing so wrong with the teenager that twenty years won't cure.

In a classroom of one genius and one idiot, over which do we waste our time?

The United States of America

> A social trap for sophisticated rodents.
> A geological net that caught all fishes.
> A place where troubled stars in the whole system
>   twinkled on one planet.
> A system that magnetized the needs of the oppressed and
>   the greedy.
> Where brothers kill brothers to impress their sisters.
> A ship that will eventually sink because of its
>   unbalanced sails.

I don't make resolutions, I may keep them.

Politics are all garbage...without the odor.

Marriage is like reading a horror story...every page.

A penny though least significant is necessary to comprise the whole.
No fertile imagination can touch the pain of reality.

Fools dream of the acquisition of fortunes; wise men make them come true.

why so quickly do we believe the lie and so reluctantly adhere to the truth?

Beauty has a tendency to slip away when you carry a frown.

Faith is lighting a candle in the dark and there is still no light.

The one thing that travels from place to place and never molested is a fruit cake.

Growing old is not for the young.

Sleep is just a short preamble of death.

What is worse than a broken condom? One that droops.

It breathes on me
It follows me
It shouts at me
Speeds toward me
Fights life with me
And the inevitable finality
It catches me.
We call it death.

The only way I was convinced of my ugliness, I had to look into the mirror.

Put to much pressure on the shell and you spoil the nut.

The woman's sure way to lose respect of a man is to say "yes".

An old man is not a fool when he spends his money on youth, but also spends it for the lack of it.

What a dejected feeling to scan an empty bottle of wine purloined of its content.

Is it not wonderful that in this game of sex that age prevents women from forever holding the winning card.

Sex in the body is not everything, but is a thing in everybody.

This is an addiction, we call greed
When we take more than we need;
And follies often praise and kid us
Surely, we cannot take it with us.

A tick, a tock, and grains of sand drop
Time, its commodity never seems to stop.

Life and time should not be measured by years but by lagging seconds.
There is congruity in every day that passes.
Yet we only live it: One day at a time.

No matter how indelible the moment seems, we can never live it again.

Never speak of a price until you are sure of the sale.

Antiquity is the only mark of beauty, but a kiss carries beauty in all ages.

Men grow old, but thoughts remain young.

The dexterity of the cook's hands marks the beauty of its taste.

Simplicity in style causes no perplexity in affection.

The permanency of a smile never has to endure the intrusion of a frown.

methodology is merely the smallest slice of a perfected pie.

Let your heavy heart carry the weight in lovable memories.

Let each tear cultivate God's strength against your grief.

Putting a tie on the tramp does not make him neater; Adding sugar to honey does not make it sweeter.

I had a roof above my head,
Had love, respect, beyond my bed,
Never was hungry by this command
From gentle strength of a husband.

Eventually, a smile will turn to frown
And tears dry up upon the ground;
All funerals, we'll soon forget
'Til those behind us are left to fret.

All of ecstasy has its penalty and pleasure admits pain,
And every ray of sunlight brings forth—unwanted rain.

We wait until the flesh shows and then we call on God.

You carry the gun, and by the gun will you be carried.

The gun has many functions, yet we choose to make it a killer.

I simply pulled the trigger—and all hell opened its doors.

The expressed orbit of time has no stops along the way.

We flush away old iniquities only to make room for the new ones.

We neither clean our bodies of all dirt, nor clean our souls of all sins.

Think! Have no compunctions at what you say or do; then there will be no regrets.

How depressing: to love in an half nurtured bed.

I accept protest
    in God's laws
And weight the test
    and all its flaws;
Abortion, in its strife
Encroaches in the womb,
Never seeing life...
An infant in its tomb.

The good thing about being Black is that the plight toward freedom is a wonderful challenge.

The arrogance of a strong nation will be its own destruction.

On our day of death and short of breath before our final nod, we glory all before our fall, then we call on God.

There are common properties of a funeral; it revives old animosities of forgotten growth; it sparks and ignites a fading of old friends; and families show the curst of their poisonous tongues in tumultuous grief, and lying in the midst of this weeping war rests the disturbed and deceased.

Technology will give man a bit of longevity before it destroys him.

If you aren't man enough to say "I am sorry", then don't be fool enough to get in that position.

The beginning and the end are so closely connected that I hardly had time to smile at my youth or to frown at my old age.

We all are engulfed with sexually and mixed similitudes...lying somewhere between man and woman.

To Blacks, God gave hope and a White man's compassion.

The greatest thing in competition is to be a winner; the least one could be is a loser; and the loneliest one could be is a bad competitor.

Whiskey is hemlock in small doses.

Once the loins have met, then Nature has nothing else to offer.

Love comes from a pocket in your heart and not the money from your pocket.

The poorest and loneliest man I know is the one who has no friends.

Action draws the footprints of a man's mind.

A rich man's wealth unwatched will eventually melt away.

Conscience can be the prisoner in the castle within you.

Beauty and ugly are all one of the same, for how could you be either without the other.

Sleep is a short interlude with a long breath.

Masturbatism: Arm weary, hand numb—ejaculation and so quick the moment is over.

God gave us an inevitable love in restructuring the process of our own kind but failed to instill upon us the morality of His laws.

How often does beauty demand the strength of a man—causing him to display his frailties.

Erection is God's way of making a penetrable play.

Sex is beautiful–the whole second.

Sex without foreplay is like dunking donuts in an empty cup.

Man is conqueror of every political and military engagement, except that of the opposing force of a woman brigade.

The beauty of sex is not in the eyes but in the loins.

What a trick of Nature: That beauty after sex— is no more.

Cracking a nut is a sweet challenge.

There is a limited reward in cracking the crab.

The taste of eating the orange is not worth sticky fingers.

I wonder if the stomach knows when you use the wrong fork.

What a distasteful dinner when you can't pick up the chicken.

The need of air is as vital to the rich as to the poor.

If nature were to divest the rich and poor of all their raiments, what would be the difference?

What a contrast of beauty when there is a contingency of <u>Black and White</u>.

<u>The sun shines on the weed as well as the rose.</u>

LaVergne, TN USA
22 August 2009
155602LV00001B/15/A